THE PERSISTENCE OF MEMORY

A Faith Interpretation of Art Forms

WILLIAM R. RAGSDALE, SR.

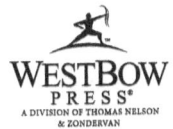

WESTBOW
PRESS®
A DIVISION OF THOMAS NELSON
& ZONDERVAN

Copyright © 2019 William R. Ragsdale, Sr.

All rights reserved. No part of this book may be used or reproduced by any means, graphic, electronic, or mechanical, including photocopying, recording, taping or by any information storage retrieval system without the written permission of the author except in the case of brief quotations embodied in critical articles and reviews.

This book is a work of non-fiction. Unless otherwise noted, the author and the publisher make no explicit guarantees as to the accuracy of the information contained in this book and in some cases, names of people and places have been altered to protect their privacy.

WestBow Press books may be ordered through booksellers or by contacting:

WestBow Press
A Division of Thomas Nelson & Zondervan
1663 Liberty Drive
Bloomington, IN 47403
www.westbowpress.com
1 (866) 928-1240

Because of the dynamic nature of the Internet, any web addresses or links contained in this book may have changed since publication and may no longer be valid. The views expressed in this work are solely those of the author and do not necessarily reflect the views of the publisher, and the publisher hereby disclaims any responsibility for them.

Any people depicted in stock imagery provided by Getty Images are models, and such images are being used for illustrative purposes only. Certain stock imagery © Getty Images.

Scripture quotations are taken from the King James Version of the Bible.

The New Testament in Modern English by J.B Phillips copyright © 1960, 1972 J. B. Phillips. Administered by The Archbishops' Council of the Church of England. Used by Permission.

ISBN: 978-1-9736-6642-4 (sc)
ISBN: 978-1-9736-6643-1 (e)

Library of Congress Control Number: 2019908011

Print information available on the last page.

WestBow Press rev. date: 7/1/2019

Also by the author, "Magic Around the World" by Bill Ragsdale, a script of a school assembly magic show. Now available at **www.magicmethods.com** and a few other magic dealers.

"Let this mind be in you, which was also in Christ Jesus:"
-*Philippians 2:5 (KJV)*

Dedicated to my wife,
Annie Joe Ivie Ragsdale

CONTENTS

1. Preface 1
2. Introduction 3
3. Foreword 5
4. Gulf Stream 7
5. The Persistence of Memory* 11
6. Avenue Q* 15
7. The King's Speech* 17
8. A Photographic Mind 21
9. A Blue, Blue, Blue, Blue Christmas* 25
10. Individual/Group Art Form Discussion Guide 29
11. Blue Suede Shoes 33
12. The Art of Magic 37
13. The Virgin Birth* 41
14. Credits 45
15. About the Author 47

PREFACE

The initial stimulus for this book came to the author in a dream early one morning the day after having visited The Dali Museum in St. Petersburg, Florida USA on May 6, 2019. This is presented in the chapter titled "The Persistence of Memory." Also, in the dream the three sayings on the cathedral in Milan, Italy came from a sermon preached by Dr Gaston Foote in the summer of 1958 when the author was working the sound system in the Stuart Auditorium at Lake Junaluska, NC.

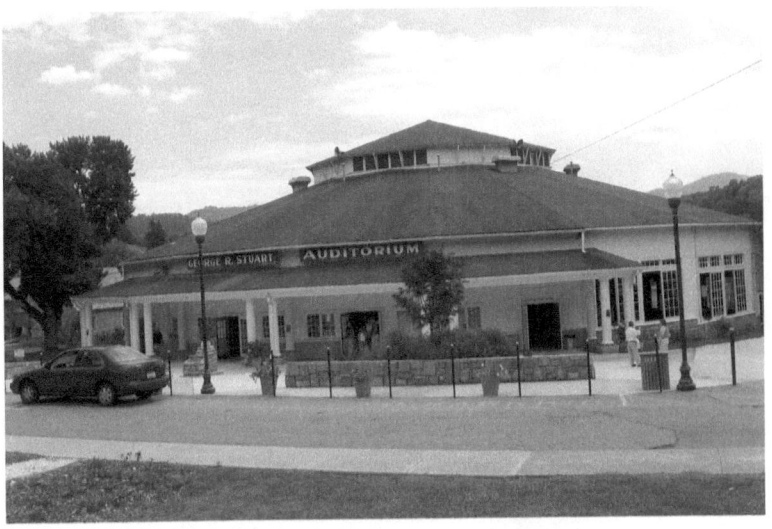

Stuart Auditorium, Lake Junaluska, NC USA- by author

INTRODUCTION

ot all forms of art are included in this book. Movies is one example, although one movie Rocketman is used as an example of using the discussion guide in the chapter "Individual/Group Art Form Discussion Guide." and 12 steps of Alcoholics Anonymous. Four of the author's favorite movies are The Sound of Music, Beverly Hills Cop, ET, and The Blues Brothers. Another example of art forms not used in this book would be more songs, like Aretha Franklin singing, Respect and Frank Sinatra singing I Did It My Way. Although one song is used Blue Suede Shoes.

However, the reader can use the art form discussion guide presented in the chapter titled "Individual/Group Art Form Discussion Guide" on the art form of their choice and make it personal by asking the questions given under each heading. The guide can also be used where there are groups of persons. The guide is used as a teaching tool to bring more depth, meaning, and growth. When this is done in a group it has been suggested that the leader go around the room allowing each person an opportunity to participate rather than letting one participant dominate and monopolize a discussion. And if a person does not want to participate verbally, then they can say "I pass." These instructions are given at the start by the leader of the group discussion.

It needs to be pointed out that The Serenity Prayer is referred to and used several times in the book mainly because it is interwoven in the author's life.

THE PERSISTENCE OF MEMORY
by William R. Ragsdale, Sr.

FOREWORD

n the often-covered Sam Cooke hit "Wonderful World," the singer (who doesn't know much about history, trigonometry or much else except his love) characterizes his reading with these words: "Looked at the pictures and I turned the pages."

What is a book, anyhow? A very long stream of words. Occasionally pictures are inserted in order to illustrate what the words are about. If you see a book has a fair number of pictures, you conclude you might get through the book more quickly than if there were none.

But what if we pondered a very different kind of book? There are words, yes. But the words are one witness's reflections on the pictures. The point of the book is to look. At the pictures, indeed, but at whatever arts, images, paintings, photographs we might encounter. Faith is a special way of seeing, isn't it?

Bill Ragsdale has gifted us with a remarkable book. Some of his favorite images are featured, such as Winslow Homer's "Gulf Stream" or Salvador Dali's "The Persistence of Memory." He jauntily and cleverly moves to other art forms: a stage play ("Avenue Q"), a movie ("The King's Speech"), a song ("Blue Suede Shoes"). He even pokes around in magic a little – and he should know, as he's dazzled a few folks with some of his own magic tricks.

The focus is never on Ragsdale, or even his words, wise and probing as they may be. Like a seasoned docent in a museum, he fixes our gaze on the art, so we look, and see, and keep seeing more. Questions matter more than answers. There is nothing dogmatic or definitive about Ragsdale's ruminations. Instead, they open wide a door for your imagination to have at it.

I wish we had more books like The Persistence of Memory, which you read slowly, or rather peruse, gaze and explore slowly. Some lingering is required, and a revisit to a previous page. And then the book's methodology lingers in us when we're out and about. We notice. We suspect. We wonder. We slow down. We think. We feel.

Thank you, Bill Ragsdale, for such a marvelous present.

Dr James Howell, **Senior Pastor**
Myers Park United Methodist Church
Charlotte, NC

GULF STREAM

It could be said that the author grew up with "Gulf Stream" by Winslow Homer. There was a knock-off copy in oil of Homer's classic painting hanging in Meadow Greens Country Club, Eden, NC, which was viewed many times; his parents took him there beginning in 1940. Glancing from time to time at the painting when taken there sort of had the effect of burning it into his mind and memory.

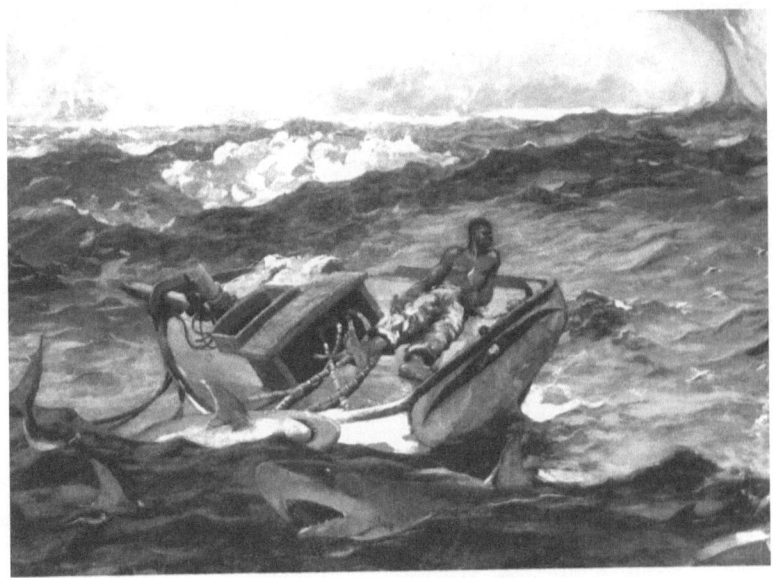

Gulf Stream by Windslow Homer, Metropolotian Museum of Art, New York City

These days, thanks to the internet, there is at least one other interpretation. It is called "aesthetic realism" which is a school of thought among artists/critics. From this interpretation we can see the man has food to eat (see the green sugar cane behind his right foot), this nourishment which will help until he gets on land or is rescued by the ship in the painting (see the ship faintly in the far left ?) This means things are not as bad as they seem for the man on the boat.

Theologically there is another way to interpret this painting. Using the Art Form Discussion Guide given in a chapter below, the author uses it and The Serenity Prayer with "Gulf Steam." The long form of "The Serenity Prayer" originally written by Reinhold Niebuhr is at the end of this chapter. It also appears in the United Methodist Hymnal. Here then is the Serenity Prayer:

> "God grant me the serenity to accept
> the things I cannot change,
> courage to change the things I can, and
> wisdom to know the difference."

Rewritten in a more direct and personal way it can be like this:

> God grant me the serenity to accept people
> I cannot stand,
> courage to change the person I can, and
> wisdom to know that person is me.

With Neibuhr's prayer as our guide, let us now look at "Gulf Stream" from the point of view of the man sitting on the boat and imagine what he could be thinking/saying/praying to himself.

God (or what the man on the boat is, was, and will be going through with his life; in other words what he is "up-against". Just look at what is around him, high wind, storm coming, sharks, etc) grant me the serenity (doesn't he look serene and peaceful ?) to accept the things I cannot change (imagine some of what he has been through: a storm or one coming (see one on upper far right), fighting sharks, and losing the sail to power the boat)

Courage (like his will is turned over to God and doesn't he look courageous? See his muscles, his bare shirtless body) to change the things I can. Moreover, wisdom to know the difference.

From the painter's point of view, it could be said this is where we are right now lying on the boat in the center of the painting. A ship with sails in the far distant left — Is it coming or going ? Past or future ? Representing hope, maybe? We do not know. Then on the right a cyclone – is it coming or going, past or future? We do not know. All we really know right now is that we are here in God's creation, His hands and all about us is coming and going. And we are just passing through. Living between the no longer and the not yet.

The Serenity Prayer which like good poetry and the Psalms in the Old Testament is quite useful at many times. Thanks to God for the painting Gulf Stream and The Serenity

Prayer for making them part of life. The long form of the prayer is given below.

Serenity Prayer

God grant me the
Serenity to accept the things
I cannot change:
Courage to change the things
I can; and
The wisdom to know the difference.
Living one day at a time;
Enjoying one moment at a time;
Accepting hardship
As the pathway to peace;
Taking as He did, this sinful
world as it is, not as I would
have it;
Trusting that He will make all things right,
if I surrender
to his will;
That I may be reasonably happy
in this life, and supremely
happy with Him forever in
the next. Amen.

- Reinhold Niebuhr

THE PERSISTENCE OF MEMORY*

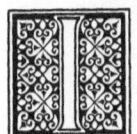n Milan, Italy, there is a cathedral, which has 3 portals/entrances. Over each portal there are three Latin phrases; translated into English they are: "All that pleases is but for the moment." "All that troubles is but for the moment." and finally over the center archway, "That only is important which is eternal." Actually today, there are 5 entrances, so historically this story of 3 portals goes back in time before any additions. Also, like all stories it is from an oral tradition probably used as an outline for a sermon or homely.

Let's think about those three phrases. First, "All that pleases is but for the moment." There are so many things that are pleasing and pleasant here in this world. To begin a list we could mention the performing arts, music and the many types of food. Then we might add hobbies, gambling, sex, flowers, pets, alcohol, sweets and the list could go on and on.

Second, "All that troubles is but for the moment." There is a gospel music song titled "Trouble In My Way" by Luther Barnes that says it all. A list of troubles could begin with death that happens in families and in society from time to time, like shootings. To mention a few more we could begin with troubles from terrorism, natural disasters like fire/flood, abuse, bankruptcy, a flat tire, trouble in family and work relationships, and this list could go on and on.

Finally, there is over the center portal "That only is important which is eternal." In St. Petersburg, Florida there is the Dali Museum built in 2011. This is a museum about the artistic work of a Catholic surrealist artist, Salvador Dali. A dominate painting there is "The Disintegration of the Persistence of Memory." (1952-54) An earlier, recognizable painting (1931) of the name "The Persistence of Memory" is in the Museum of Modern Art in New York City. Each painting shows three bent melting watches. However, each one has a different landscape and the later painting 1952-54 has the word "disintegration" added to the title, which suggests some growth and growing-up might have happened for Mr. Dali. Also, it is noted the landscapes are different which suggests life today is broken. What are these paintings pointing to ? What do they suggest ? Say?

A faith/theological answer might be they are pointing to a place where time is of no use, where time does not work, namely the other world, or heaven.

> Lay not up for yourselves treasures upon earth, where moth and rust doth corrupt, and where thieves break through and steal: But lay up for yourselves treasures in heaven, where neither

moth nor rust doth corrupt, and where thieves do not break through nor steal.
Matthew 6:19-20 KJV

This is the place we pray for, to be here on earth in The Lord's Prayer. It is the place where the creating God Almighty is and the risen/living spirit of Jesus is in us and among us in this world. May this continue daily in our memory.

*First printed in The Salisbury Post newspaper, Salisbury, NC USA

AVENUE Q*

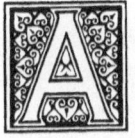venue Q as a whole is one of the best sermons the author had seen and heard in a long time, but not in the traditional manner like the way sermons are given in churches Sunday after Sunday or whenever. The musical Avenue Q was beautifully presented in the Norvell Theater in Salisbury, NC. It was well put together. It uses hand-held puppets, which made it appealing to all adult-children, the child within all adults.

Like in many churches there is a prayer of confession in their order of worship. This is presented in Avenue Q in several songs; below three are interpretations.

First, there is the song "It Sucks To Be Me" a song sung twice. Paul in Romans 7 described this insight into ourselves that we are - each of us - sinful or separated: "Yet if I do things that I don't really want to do then it is not, I repeat, "I" who do them, but the sin which has made it home within me." (J.B. Phillips translation) Paul Tillich put it this way in his sermon "You Are Accepted"; "he who has learned to over-come self-contempt has overcome his contempt for others."

Then there is song "Everybody's A Bit Racist Sometime." This is true regardless of our original race or color. This corporate confessional piece performed in an artistic manner - musical - packs a punch !

Thirdly, sin is dealt with musically in the song "Schadenfreude" – about happiness at the misfortune of others. Paul Tillich in a sermon mentioned above wrote in the 1940's: "Today we can confirm what Immanuel Kant, the prophet of human reason and dignity was honest enough to say: there is something about the misfortune of our best friends which does not displease us."

There is much more to understand and unpack in this musical art form but it is not possible in a short time at 3 in the morning. Yes, it was offensive, but the Gospel of Jesus Christ continues to be offensive to some people.

A very significant topic raised in Avenue Q is the song "PURPOSE." The answer to the purpose of mankind is given in the Westminster Catechism "To praise God and enjoy Him forever."

*First printed in The Salisbury Post newspaper 2018, Salisbury, NC USA

THE KING'S SPEECH*

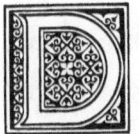uring a lecture at Duke Divinity School's 2013 convocation for pastors, chaplains and other graduates, a lecturer used a recent movie The King's Speech as an illustration. Much of the lecture which was really quite good and written in red in the notes taken was the word healing. The movie is about healing. Simple as it sounds, this is true.

Come to think of it, that's what the gospels tell us over and over that Jesus was doing in the New Testament, that is, healing the broken and crushed spirits of people He met. And through the risen spirit of Jesus it is happening all around us day in and day out these days in groups and people reaching out to help others, like Hospice, Overeaters Anonymous, The Red Cross, Narcotics Anonymous, Gamblers Anonymous, Alcoholics Anonymous, Sex Anonymous, Emotions Anonymous, and there many more that could be named, like first responders at accidents and fires. Healing is beautifully displayed in the movie The King's Speech.

After much reflection and thought this awareness about healing has become clear both in the movie and in lives about us. First, the movie begins with King George VI of England who has a stuttering problem. Enter a speech therapist who begins the process of helping the King with his problem. This is a lengthy process taking many frustrating weeks and months. During this time the therapist gets King George to look at the events in his family of origin in which he grew up as a child. What is discovered as he looks at an event and at himself, there are emotions blocking the King's spirit? The present day stuttering of the King is the result of blocking emotions and not facing or dealing with them. Once the king faces this head on he is better able to deal with his stuttering problem and give critical public speeches.

A young man who had a problem with his own anger and resentment presented it to his counselor. The counselor suggested that for healing to begin to happen that the young man look within his family of origin. Over time this is what happens in the movie The King's Speech as the King guided by the therapist is able to deliver a power radio speech.

Anger is not an emotion that is easily discussed in society back in the 1940's and earlier. It was, sort of a hush – hush topic or taboo issue that was not brought out in the open. These days it is still not discussed in some circles. Depending upon who you talk with now it is more out in the open. Just as King George was helped by the speech therapist with his issues there has been help and continues to be help for persons with anger and resentment from clergy, counselors, Drs, therapists, and others. For many persons the help comes from a Power greater than themselves. That Power is God

Almighty, the God of Creation. He is the One who operates the seasons of the year – winter, spring, summer and fall.

Today there are times when anger comes up for all of us.. When it happens praying humbly and silently in our minds, to the God of Creation usually works over time. It needs to be done on a daily basis. The anger does not always immediately go away but continuing to pray to God and working with others anger is given a back seat.

Anger happens all around us in society sometimes in violent ways and other times in non-violent ways. Look at the terrorism and violence around the world. Yet it is usually and wrongly thought "I can handle it." The truth is we cannot handle it alone. Will power alone is useless. We need a Power greater than us, namely God and Jesus Christ. Slowly but surely various agencies are at work analyzing and coming up with solutions as we of all faiths bring about healing and salvation in the world today.

*First printed in The Salisbury Post newspaper (2011), Salisbury, NC USA

A PHOTOGRAPHIC MIND

Or Being in This World (earth) and The Other World (heaven) simultaneously

A poetical art form given at 3 am by a hospital nurse was "You have a photographic mind, but no film." Sort of like trying to fully understand the Christian faith or any faith is like "trying to nail jello to the wall." Where the nurse got the phrase is not known; she probably made it up herself as the author talked and talked and talked and talked in the dead of the night. The poetical phrase was most likely an observation the nurse made of the author running his mouth. Sometimes we can go off track as Christians.

The other world or "film" is the foundation of our faith in God and the living Jesus Christ. Often times we get distracted by events in this world by the troubles or pleasures we live with daily. There is a lot of struggling and pain in this world where we are called to be of service by God and Jesus. The author was called to be of service as a chaplain at the N.C. State Veterans Home in Salisbury, N.C. where he served for just over 14 years. One memorable bedside visit was with a veteran who had had a stroke and was left paralyzed on one side of his body, but he could verbalize and talk. The chaplain had talked and joked many times with him and his roommate who listened many times to the jokes. These were clean jokes gotten off the Internet.

Well, this veteran was confused nearing the end over his situation about being paralyzed and being unable to walk even though he was being given therapy, he also became confused as was pointed out by a nurse and confirmed by all three of us, the veteran, the nurse, and the chaplain. It occurred what might help him at this time was The Serenity Prayer. He was asked if he had ever heard of The Serenity Prayer. He said no. So we prayed it together after it was verbally recited for him. He seemed to like the prayer. The reality and truth was this veteran might never walk again and all the therapy was really not going to help him actually walk. So back in the office the prayer was written out on a piece of copy paper.

> God grant me the serenity to accept
> the things I cannot change
> Courage to change the things I can
> And wisdom to know the difference.

On the next visit the veteran read over the paper and what was written on it and said "put that on my bulletin board." The prayer mean something to him and he found it helpful or he wanted to remember it. Within a few weeks, he passed on.

Sometimes in visits the Holy Bible was read often in the King James Version or whatever version was handy. Isaiah 40:31 was also a big help. "Those who wait on the Lord shall renew their strength, they shall mount up on wings as eagles, then shall run and not be weary, they shall walk and not faint, help us Lord, help us Lord in thy way" The last words come from a song based on Isaiah 40:31. This was done to help us all work on our patience in this fast moving world with computers, iPhones, and other electronic gadgets.

The "no film" part of the phrase "You have a photographic mind, but no film." is best understood as being not connected mentally in faith to God and Jesus. It means we all get caught up in family relationships when things happen like death, divorce, bankruptcy, drug/alcohol abuse, and a host of things distract us from our faith. Sometimes we get angry and have to "go sit in the corner" as adult-children physically removing ourselves from whatever has disturbed our peace and serenity. Then as time moves us along we become more balanced living on earth and heaven with God and Jesus at the same time. So let us be grateful for this faith living among us and have an "attitude of gratitude" being thankful.

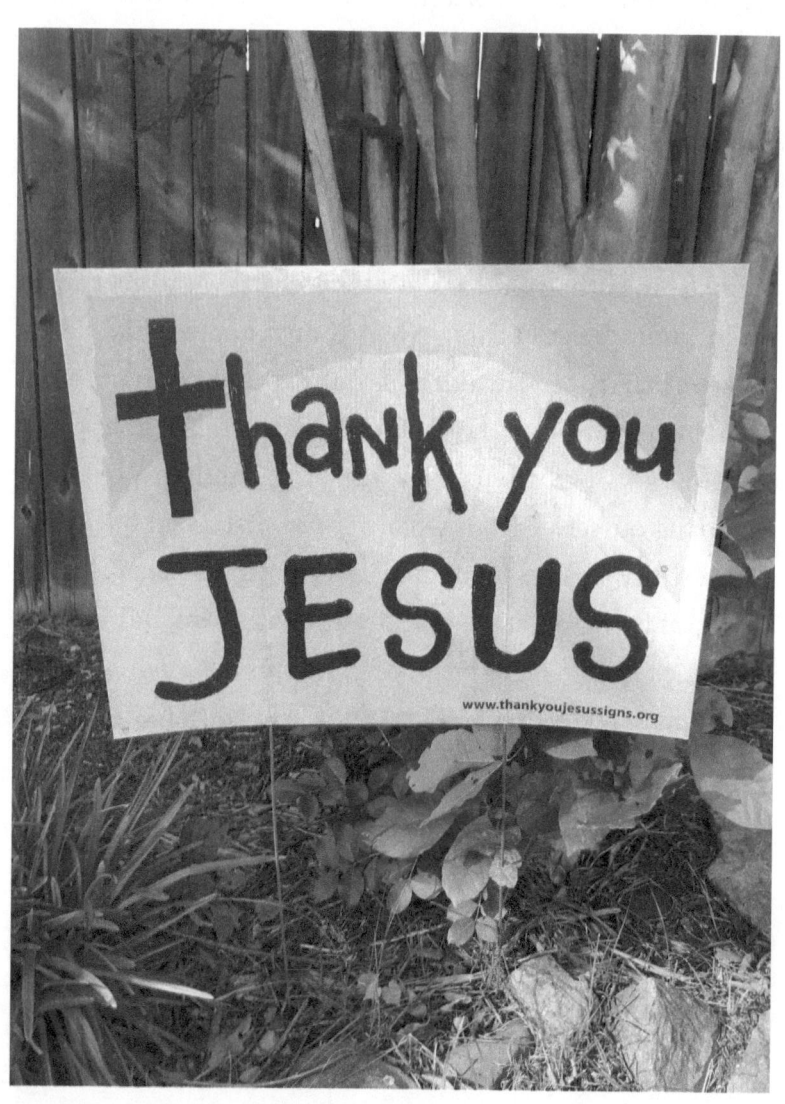

A BLUE, BLUE, BLUE, BLUE CHRISTMAS*

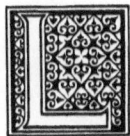istening to Rufus Wainwright and Lou Reed sing "Blue Christmas" made me realize there are many people around us daily who have recently lost a loved one. They will be having a blue Christmas adjusting to this change in life about them.

You can hear Lou and Rufus sing the song on You Tube or if you prefer, listen to Elvis sing it; he made it popular years ago. Just go to You Tube and type in either name or "Blue Christmas," if you have a computer or iPad. Now these days we have a computer that fits in our hands, it's the iPhone.

Who among us has not had a blue Christmas thinking about relatives and friends who have died and passed on? There is hardly anyone among us who does not have persons close to us in our memories and this song "Blue Christmas" takes on a really powerful significance.

Most of us have dealt with our parents who have passed on and are now having a "white" Christmas in Heaven as expressed in Jim Reeves' lyrics of the song. The real calling is how can we be of help to those living about us in our lives today who have lost loved ones.

To answer this calling means we have a plan for dealing with grief and mourning. There are several things we can do.

First, we need to deal with our own grief over the death/loss of a loved one be that a mother, father, or other close relative. We could begin with our own pastor or find one and ask if he/she can help us. Then there is Hospice, which we could contact for grief counselors and support groups.

Support groups can be most helpful if a person is having a particularly difficult time with a loss. In a grief support group a person can find strength from others who have also lost a loved one.

Secondly, we might also have an Intercessory prayer for them by praying to God. Thirdly, we can listen to them — not talk, but let them talk. Fourth, we could share with them how we have handled our own grief and loss.

During my days in seminary in the mid 1960's I learned of a booklet that was most helpful. Since that time, the booklet has been printed and reprinted over and over. It is Granger Westburg's Good Grief. Then there are other books and pamphlets like "Care Notes" which come at loss from a variety of directions.

Perhaps the starting point might be to ask God and Christ to guide us and help us as we deal with "Blue Christmas" for ourselves as well as others.

Here are Jim Reeves' lyrics to "Blue Christmas."

> I'll have a blue Christmas without you
> I'll be so blue just thinking about you

Decorations of red on a green Christmas tree
Won't be the same dear, if you're not here with me
And when those blue snowflakes start fallin'
That's when those blue heartaches start callin'
You'll be doin' all right with you Christmas of white
But I'll have a blue, blue, Christmas

*First printed in The Salisbury Post newspaper (2017), Salisbury, NC USA

INDIVIDUAL/GROUP ART FORM DISCUSSION GUIDE

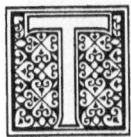he guide below was first written for use with a group of people to get to a depth understand how an art form essentially could be understood from a faith point of view. Namely, the Christian faith, but this is not to exclude Jewish, Muslim, Buddhist and other faiths. It was first used in the 1960's; it is from The Ecumenical Institute: Chicago which evolved into The Institute of Cultural Affairs or ICA where the author interned in the early 1970's for 4 years.

The Individual/Group Discussion Guide can be used on all art forms from theatre, movies, ballet, music, etc. Also, it can be used by a single individual as is revealed in other chapters in this book. For sure, other chapters of this book are examples of one person using the guide to offer a faith interpretation. The method has four types of questions. They are impressionistic, reflective, interpretative, and faith questions. This last group of questions can be changed depending on your faith stance or religious point of view. The author's faith is Christian. Also, the guide can be used in a purely secular fashion without using the fourth theological or faith part.

The procedure begins with a rapid movement around the group one person at a time giving each person an opportunity to share or pass and be quiet. One person in the group is given a finger gun to shoot down any rabbits or talk that goes off the targeted art form. If needed ask a person to recall the first 3-5 responses to make sure everyone is listening!

Moving along through the questions it gets deeper and the responses are longer. Involvement will increase verbally and participation is slower. The leader should be sensitive to rhythm and pace of the discussion and know when to move from one set of questions to the other. He/she should not approve or disapprove of any answers. The leader is only the guide and does not need to offer his/her opinion or point of view unless asked or his/her words would move the group around a block. Extraneous data: like behavior or intrusions need to be blocked off so everyone can focus the discussion on the art form. This guide is most helpful with movies, drama, musicals, and paintings to name a few.

The questions consider whether the art form affects our eyes, ears, or both and whether the art form is static or dynamic. The questions below are only suggestive to help persons move to a more meaningful treatment of art forms rather than one that is trite and superficial.

Sample IMPRESSIONISTIC objective questions sort of like recalling the facts are "What do or did you see here?" "What colors do you see?" "What is the center of attention?"

"Are there any scenes that you recall which have not been mentioned?" "What music/songs do you recall?" "Sounds?" "Words?" Phrases?" "Scenes without music or with music?" This is just getting the facts out like Jack Webb in the TV Show "Dragnet."

Moving along in-group discussion the REFLECTIVE questions are like these: How does this make you feel? What is the atmosphere of the picture? Where did you feel happiest? saddest? What character did you identify with? What actions do you imagine going on here? (This question is helpful if sculpture or a painting is used.) What would you add or take out?

The next level of questions are the INTERPRETATIVE ones. Like, what is the most important part? What story would you tell about this _____? What has happened here? What is the most important part? What is going on? What one word is coming out of the art form? If you could, what one word or phrase would you say to this art form? What is the problem presented here? Where do you see this going on in the world today?

THEOLOGICAL/FAITH

Where do you see God at work or "up-against-ness" happening? Where do you see sin or separation reflected? Where do you see grace happening or a Damascus road event happening? or change going on ? Where do you see the Christ event happening or new/risen life happening?

Now let's put the guide to use with a current movie, namely Rocketman about the life of Elton John seen by the author on June 1, 2019. Going directly to the faith questions we realize that this movie is an example of a Damascus Road event or a Christ event as given in Acts 9 where Paul is changed. At the start of the movie when Elton John is in rehab for his alcohol and drug abuse he says, "I'm an alcoholic." Then at the end of the movie, we see pictures of a saved and redeemed Elton 28 years sober with his family including two adopted children. Stay in focus now on Elton and not slip on to his homosexuality and partner which is like chasing a rabbit and also, controversial. We can see he has changed in the movie. We do not see what has happened in the process, in between, from the start to the end of the movie. It could be assumed in rehab the 12 steps of Alcoholics Anonymous played a part given his 28 years sober! The 12 steps came out the Oxford Group first intended to help Christians be better Christians.

BLUE SUEDE SHOES

hat was Carl Perkins writing about and Elvis Presley singing when they wrote and sang to us "Don't Step on My Blue Suede Shoes"?

They were somehow trying to say I'll be who I am and you be who you are without stepping over the line. "On my blue suede shoes." In other words to be positive, let's respect each other and be courteous to one another. Sort of like Rodney King when he asked "Why can't we just get along?"

Much of why we step on each other's blue suede shoes has to do with our individual histories and our growing up in families of origin where some of us had an abusive childhood, some real bad, some only moderately bad, and some pretty good. To varying degrees each of us have had childhoods that have been sometimes rather good and sometimes bad; to put it bluntly where the abuse may have only been moderate, like some verbal abuse that is passed off as "I was only teasing" compared to that of those who have had extreme physical abuse and sexual abuse. Now today we show up trying to do the best we can carrying the baggage of our different histories, memories and pasts.

It has to do with stepping on each other's blue suede shoes

or to be precise, in other words, stepping on each other's rights as individuals. All this is because many of us do not really stop and think with our minds what Jesus was saying when he gave us the commandment to love others as we love ourselves. We just assume we love ourselves. The truth is lots of the time we don't. And if we do, it is usually only half way or merely in part. If we really loved ourselves, we might simply keep our mouths shut when we are up against someone who is totally or in part different from ourselves or with whom we disagree.

Loving and caring for ourselves from God's point of view can happen when we do a personal inventory and start or even continue to work on letting God help each of us correct some of our character defects and shortcomings. To do this we have to be honest with ourselves. We have some work to do, each of us to be true to ourselves. We have to be honest with ourselves. It will help us from stepping on others blue suede shoes and rights.

To help from stepping on others rights we have topics to discuss like the weather and the seasons of the year that we find ourselves involved in and cannot vote on, influence or change. These are at least two topics we can discuss politely with just about anyone. Like, what is your favorite season of the year ? There are others but this one comes to mind quickly, and it is certainly not controversial issue where people are constantly stepping on the rights of others, not to mention their own rights. Other questions can be easily thought of.

There are a couple of other concerns that are rather important for these days. One is healing and the other is growing or learning. Right now for the time being most of us are working on and under construction with how we keep from stepping on others blue suede shoes (rights). This may be hard at times -the easy way out would be to make a snappy judgment or act in an uncompromising or rigid way.

A big help with this is praying to God Almighty and the spirit of the on-going healer Jesus !

THE ART OF MAGIC

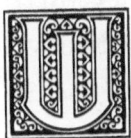ith the printing of "The Art of Magic" postage stamps in the USA, it is clear that magic is an art form.

"The purpose of art is washing the dust off our souls." Pablo Picasso. "You can use a glass mirror to see your face; you use works of art to see your soul." George Bernard Shaw.

Anyone who has seen a performance of Harry Blackstone, Jr., Lance Burton, Jeff McBride, David Copperfield, or Siegfried & Roy has encountered a performing art form of sheer mystery and wonder. There are thousands less well-known performing magicians and this is happening in other countries around the world. These more popular and well-known magicians have done lots and lots of rehearsing (practice) because a magician is merely an actor playing the part of a magician.

Many of these close-up magicians can be seen on the Penn and Teller TV show, like Paul Gertner who has appeared several times. When we see a magician and he or she has fooled us, we can't figure out how it is done what have we run into? We have run into mystery, awe, and wonder. We are reminded of the word mystery that appears in the Baltimore

Catechism many, many times! Even in the Holy Bible: And He said unto them, "Unto you is given to know the mystery of the kingdom of God: but unto them that are without, all these things are done in parables." Mark 4:11 KJV

This is just one example where the word mystery appears over 40 times in the Bible.

Taking an effect that has been presented and can still be seen in various magical shows is sawing a woman in two. We can surely understand that this an example of death and life as in the end of the effect the girl steps out healed and whole again. Just so we believe in the risen living spirit of Jesus living in this world in many ways.

It is alright if we don't understand we can still be entertained, laugh and enjoy. Then there is the magician pulling a rabbit out of a hat which is to say the future is open, "all life is open, embrace the future with vision, die your death for the living, the mystery has received all." (These words from a song sung at The Ecumenical Institute: Chicago)

Other venues of magic are comedy and mental to mention a couple more. When comedy magic is presented, we can laugh and be mystified at the same time. With mental magic we are truly amazed!

And if we can't figure magic out, then that is alright. The words of a friend, Jack Daniels, come to mind "Some things I understand, and some things I don't understand, and then I understand that I don't understand, and that's O.K."

We don't have to understand everything, just believe, have faith, trust in God & Jesus.

In a sense then when we are fooled by the magician, he/she has reminded us of the Ultimate Mystery: God, in whom we trust.

THE VIRGIN BIRTH*

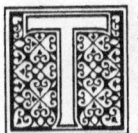he author grew up as a child spending his summers in a Methodist family at Lake Junaluska in Western NC where he was exposed to the teachings of the church living where it was called, at that time, The Lake Junaluska Methodist Assembly grounds. Around 14 years of age he was having an especially difficult time struggling with how to rationally believe in the virgin birth. It was a concept he could not figure out. His mother suggested he talk with Dr. Mason Crumb who taught religion at Duke University and lived just a block from his grandfather's home at the Lake. An important symbol there is the cross which is lighted at night

suggesting God and Jesus are watching over us even as we sleep. And indeed they are when we think of the thousands of first responders as in police, fire, and medics around the world.

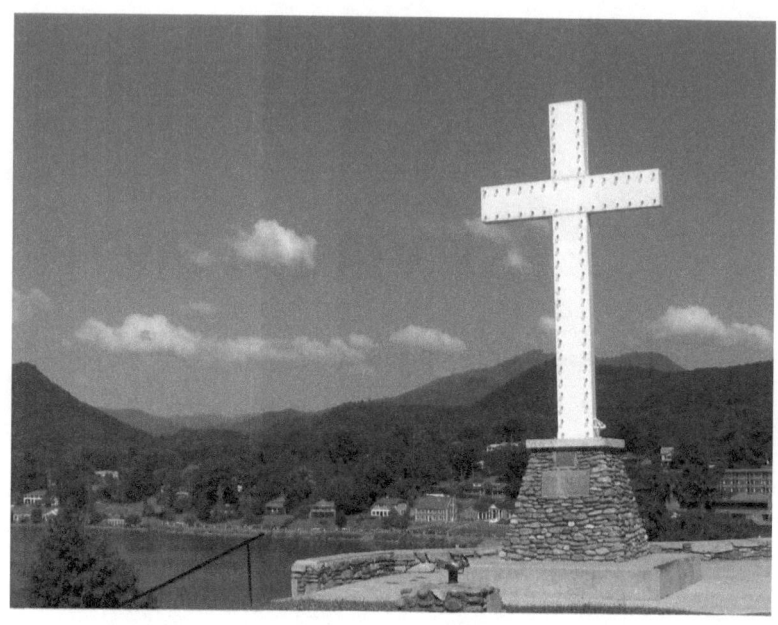

The cross at Lake Junaluska, N.C. USA - by the author

After presenting the problem to Dr. Crumb he offered a few words and finally said, "Don't throw the baby out with the bath water." In other words don't give up on a concept simply because you do not understand it.

These days the author has come to believe in the virgin birth because he has experienced it many times in his own life. Each time it has happened with varying degrees of intensity as he grew and learned one day at a time what it means to be Christian.

As protestants we have much to learn from our Catholic and Orthodox brothers and sisters. Mystery is interwoven into their faith and belief. Several times the author has worshipped in Orthodox churches where there is incense, chanting, and icons surrounding him and he experienced the awe and presence of the eternal in the midst of this world. Mystery surrounds our Christian faith. In The Baltimore Catechism used by Catholics the word "mystery" appears quite often. Indeed at one point it states: "A supernatural mystery is a truth which we cannot fully understand, but which we firmly believe because we have God's word for it." (Lesson Number 3, item 34)

This means we don't have to understand everything in order to believe it. It is sort of like driving a car. We don't have to understand what makes it work in order to drive it. In a similar way there are computers. We don't have to know and understand how one works in order to use it.

It is quite close and similar to being "born again" from above as told in John 3 in the story of Jesus and Nichodemus. Don't ask to explain how it is to be understood. It happens in our heart and soul. It is a matter of faith, a matter of belief. It is not something that can be rationally explained.

Many times in our lives we experience being born again as our personal world has been enlarged and we have grown a bit more in being Christian. Each time it happens, we find ourselves learning some new truth about our life and the lives of others. It happens when we stop behaving one way and start behaving in another, as in being more positive and not quite so negative. Today we need to be attentive to where God is active in life around us and where He would have us lay down our lives in service for others. Every time we go to sleep at night we die to the day and are born again into a new day. Being born again happens over and over in life as we continue to learn and grow. It is a matter of faith and happens in our hearts. Truly we have experienced a virgin birth in our own lives as we move through night into day!

Meister Eckhart put it in a question this way, "What good is it that Christ was born 2,000 years ago if he is not born now in your heart?" So a few years ago the author wrote a poem which expresses this:

Have A Virgin Birth

Have a virgin birth yourself
This Christmas
Let baby Jesus be born afresh
In your heart.
Quit looking around you
At the ills of
other souls.
Stop blaming others for the
Misery you have brought upon
Yourself.
Examine your own life in an honest
manner.
Talk to your heavenly Father
About this.
And have a virgin birth in
Your own heart this Christmas.

*First printed in The Salisbury Post newspaper (2015), Salisbury, NC USA

CREDITS

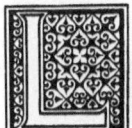et me thank those who behind the scenes have helped make this book possible. Annette Norwood and Shaina Buckles Harkness at the Dali Museum, St Petersburg, Florida, Kathy Lester, Camille Lauren and all the staff at Westbow Press, Tim Coffey photographer, and my wife for her guidance/support.

ABOUT THE AUTHOR

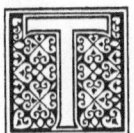he author a graduate of Hampden Sydney College, Hampden Sydney, Virginia and Duke Divinity School, Durham, NC is a retired United Methodist preacher, chaplain, and magician. He lives with his wife in Salisbury, NC.

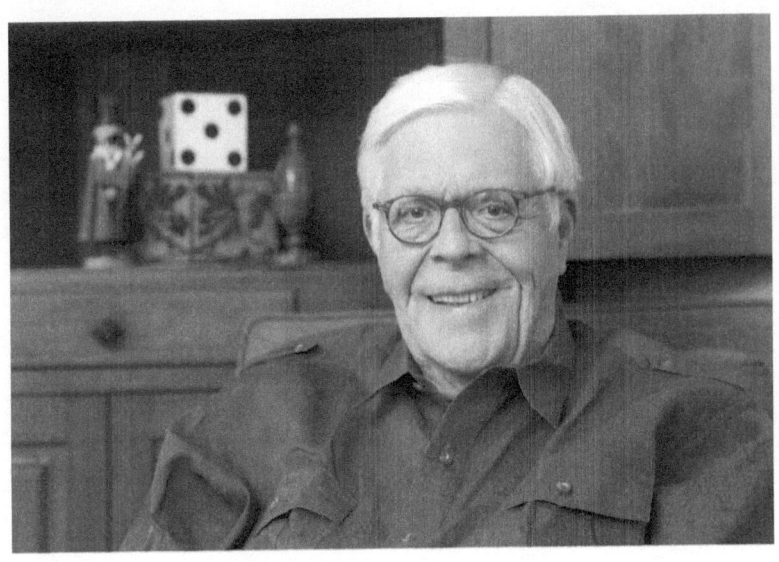

Tim Coffey photography

www.ingramcontent.com/pod-product-compliance
Lightning Source LLC
Chambersburg PA
CBHW031548210526
45464CB00003B/1210